STECK-VAUGHN
PORTRAIT OF AMERICA

Tennessee

Steck-Vaughn Company

Executive Editor	Diane Sharpe
Senior Editor	Martin S. Saiewitz
Design Manager	Pamela Heaney
Photo Editor	Margie Foster
Electronic Cover Graphics	Alan Klemp

Proof Positive/Farrowlyne Associates, Inc.
Program Editorial, Revision Development, Design, and Production

Consultant: Lorene Lambert, Travel Writer, Tennessee Tourist Development

Published by Raintree Steck-Vaughn Publishers, an imprint of Steck-Vaughn Company.

A Turner Educational Services, Inc. book. Based on the Portrait of America television series by R. E. (Ted) Turner.

Cover Photo: Great Smoky Mountains National Park by © Charles Krebs/The Stock Market.

Library of Congress Cataloging-in-Publication Data

Thompson, Kathleen.
    Tennessee / Kathleen Thompson.
       p.   cm. — (Portrait of America)
    "Based on the Portrait of America television series"—T.p. verso.
    "A Turner book."
    Includes index.
    ISBN 0-8114-7388-0 (library binding).—ISBN 0-8114-7469-0 (softcover)
    1. Tennessee—Juvenile literature. I. Title II. Series:
Thompson, Kathleen. Portrait of America.
F436.3.T46 1996
976.8—dc20

                                    95-45440
                                        CIP
                                        AC

Printed and Bound in the United States of America

3 4 5 6 7 8 9 10 WZ 03 02 01 00

Acknowledgments
The publishers wish to thank the following for permission to reproduce photographs:
P. 7 © Comstock; p. 8 The Hermitage; p. 11 (top) Tennessee State Library and Archives, (bottom) Washington University Gallery of Art, St. Louis; p. 12 (top) © Gary Layda, (bottom) National Portrait Gallery, Smithsonian Institution; p. 13 (top) Alabama Department of Archives and History, (bottom) Tennessee State Library and Archives; p. 14 National Portrait Gallery, Smithsonian Institution; p. 15 Tennessee State Library and Archives; p. 16 Tennessee State Museum; p. 17 (top) Nebraska State Historical Society, (bottom) Tennessee Valley Authority; p. 18 National Archives; p. 19 Tennessee Tourist Development; p. 20 Movie Still Archives; p. 21 (both) Tennessee Tourist Development; p. 22 Nissan; p. 24 Tennessee Tourist Development; p. 25 State of Tennessee Photographic Services; p. 26 St. Jude Hospital, Memphis; p. 27 Federal Express; p. 29 (top) Saturn Corporation, (bottom) Nissan; p. 30 Memphis Convention and Visitors Bureau; p. 32 (top) Courtesy of the Library, Phillips Exeter Academy, (bottom) © Gary Layda; p. 33 (top) Center for Southern Folklore Archive, (bottom) Memphis Convention and Visitors Bureau; p. 34 Memphis Convention and Visitors Bureau; p. 35 (top) Nashville Convention and Visitors Bureau, (bottom) Memphis Convention and Visitors Bureau; p. 36 Nashville Convention and Visitors Bureau; p. 37 Tennessee Tourist Development; p. 38 © Donnie Beauchamp/Opryland; p. 39 (top) Grand Ole Opry Archives, (bottom) Tennessee Tourist Development; pp. 40, 41 (both) Museum of Appalachia; p. 42 © Superstock; p. 44 Nashville Convention and Visitors Bureau; p. 46 One Mile Up; p. 47 (left) One Mile Up, (middle, right) Tennessee Tourist Development.

STECK-VAUGHN
PORTRAIT OF AMERICA

Tennessee

Kathleen Thompson

A Turner Book

RSVP

RAINTREE
STECK-VAUGHN
PUBLISHERS
The Steck-Vaughn Company

Austin, Texas

Tennessee

Reelfoot Lake

• Tiptonville

Clarksville

Cumberland R.

APPALACHIAN
MOUNTAINS

CUMBERLAND GAP
NATIONAL HISTORIC PARK

Kingsport

NASHVILLE ⭐

Oak Ridge

• Norris

Johnson City

Mississippi River

Ripley

Smyrna

Tennessee River

Knoxville

Henning

Jackson

• Smithville

Clingman's Dome

Memphis

• Murfreesboro

Pulaski

Chattanooga

GREAT SMOKY MOUNTAINS
NATIONAL PARK

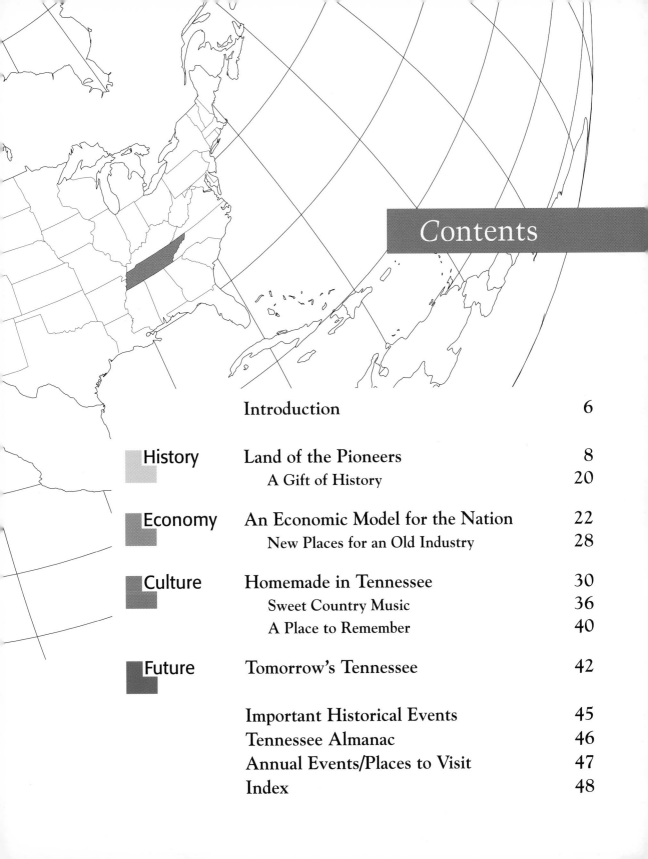

Contents

Introduction

Tennessee has done things its own way. The people who followed Daniel Boone through the Cumberland Gap were forerunners of a mountain culture that still thrives in Tennessee. Isolated from the eastern colonies by the Appalachian Mountains, the people of Tennessee learned to rely on themselves. They're independent. In fact, they're unique. Just listen to the rich twang of the fiddles at the Grand Ole Opry, center of American country music. Or wrap yourself in a colorful, hand-stitched Tennessee quilt. These are Tennessee traditions, but there's more to the state—much more. This is a modern, prosperous state with thriving industry. Blending progress with a strong grasp of the past, Tennessee has given itself a head start on the future.

Memphis has always relied on the Mississippi River, from the days of the paddlewheels before the Civil War to today, when barges carry goods to the Gulf of Mexico.

Tennessee

The Cumberland Plateau, Grand Ole Opry

Land of the Pioneers

By the time European explorers arrived in present-day Tennessee, the area was inhabited by Native American groups such as the Cherokee and the Chickasaw. The Cherokee lived in what is now middle and eastern Tennessee. They lived in small villages of log houses, and they hunted mostly deer, bear, and elk. They also cultivated maize (corn), beans, and squash.

Western Tennessee was settled by the Chickasaw. These people had conquered many other Native American groups in the area before the Europeans arrived. Instead of living in villages, the Chickasaw built temporary campsites along the rivers. They never stayed long enough in one area to grow their own food. They lived on what they could gather from the forests.

Hernando de Soto and his party of Spanish explorers were the first known Europeans to enter present-day Tennessee. They passed through looking for gold in 1540. On their way, they raided a number of Native American groups and traded with other groups.

The Hermitage, which is located outside of Nashville, was Andrew Jackson's plantation home. The building was completed in 1819.

One hundred forty years later, English and French explorers traveled the area separately. England and France struggled against each other for trade and Native Americans' lands. Small battles were taking place all over the eastern part of North America. In 1754, these battles developed into the full-scale French and Indian War. The Cherokee and the Chickasaw sided with the British, while the Creek in the south fought along with the French. In 1763 the French surrendered and recognized the British claims to all North American land that lay east of the Mississippi River.

Settlers began coming into the Tennessee area by the 1770s, taking more and more land away from the Cherokee. The number of settlers in the area grew to about one thousand. Present-day Tennessee was actually a part of North Carolina at this time, but mountains separated the pioneers from the more populous part of the colony. The pioneers felt abandoned by the colonial government, so they decided to form a government of their own in 1772, called the Watauga Association. This association was one of the first colonial attempts at establishing a constitutional government.

Meanwhile American colonists were taking action to break away from Great Britain. In 1775 the Revolutionary War began. Most of the people living in Tennessee supported the war, but not many Tennesseans actually fought in it. Most of the battles took place in the more heavily settled areas near the Atlantic Coast. So Tennesseans went about their own business of expanding their settlements.

That same year the Transylvania Land Company bought land from the Cherokee that included parts of Tennessee and Kentucky. The company sent Daniel Boone into this western wilderness to clear trails for new settlers. He began in Virginia, cut across the mountains at a valley called the Cumberland Gap, and ended up in western Tennessee. Boone's trail became known as the Wilderness Road.

A treaty to end the Revolutionary War was signed in 1783. One year later, North Carolina offered part of its western region to the federal government. This area included the eastern portion of present-day Tennessee. Before the government could accept, however, North Carolina withdrew the offer, leaving the area without any government. The settlers in the area decided to form their own state, which they called Franklin, in honor of Benjamin Franklin. North Carolina gained control of Franklin in 1788, and a year later gave it up to the federal government again. Congress referred to the area as the Territory of the United States South of the River Ohio. The area became part of Tennessee in 1796 when Tennessee became the sixteenth state to join

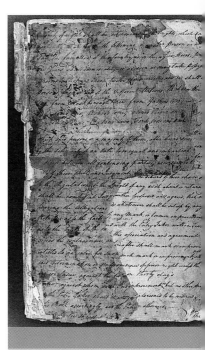

This fragment is part of the Cumberland Compact, an outline of government written by the settlers of Fort Nashborough in 1780.

This nineteenth-century painting shows Daniel Boone leading settlers through the Cumberland Gap on the Wilderness Road.

This is a reconstruction of a cabin at Fort Nashborough, the settlement that became Nashville.

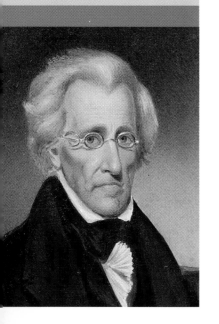

Andrew Jackson was the first Tennessean to become President of the United States. Jackson became a national hero in the War of 1812, when he led American troops at the Battle of New Orleans.

the Union. There already were over 70,000 people living in the state by that time and it grew quickly. By 1810 the population was more than 250,000.

Andrew Jackson moved from the Carolinas to Tennessee. He was elected President in 1828. The people of Tennessee were naturally proud of their "native son." He was the first President who grew up west of the Appalachian Mountains. He was raised in a log cabin. This rugged background played a large part in Jackson's identity with the nation. He was called the "people's President" because his legislation stood up for the country's farmers and workers.

There were many people, especially Native Americans, whom Jackson chose not to help. By the time he was elected President, many of Tennessee's Cherokee had taken on European ways. Some owned shops and even plantations. A Cherokee named Sequoya had developed an alphabet for the Cherokee language. But President Jackson didn't care how hard the Native Americans were trying to fit in. He wanted the Native Americans to leave so that more settlers could take over the land. In 1830 Jackson approved the Indian Removal Act. This act stated that Native Americans living east of the Mississippi River had to move to Oklahoma.

Many Native Americans ignored the act and stayed on their land. So in 1838 the government brought in troops to force them out. Their journey is now called the Trail of Tears. Most had to walk the entire way, and many were even put in handcuffs. About four thousand Cherokee died from disease, starvation, and exhaustion on the journey that covered over 800 miles.

above. General Andrew Jackson fought in many battles against Native Americans. Here, Creek leader Red Eagle surrenders to Jackson after a battle in Alabama.

below. James K. Polk was the eleventh President of the United States and the second from Tennessee.

The eleventh President of the United States, James K. Polk, took office in 1845. Polk had moved to Tennessee with his family when he was 11 years old. Before becoming President, Polk had been Tennessee's governor. Before that time, he had served 14 years in Congress. As President, Polk led the country in the Mexican War. Tennessee sent almost thirty thousand soldiers to fight, about ten times as many volunteers as the federal government required. People called Tennessee the Volunteer State, a nickname that the state is still known by today.

Andrew Johnson, who eventually became the seventeenth President of the United States, also had a long political history with the state. He began his career in local politics. Afterward, he served in the United States Congress for ten years starting in 1843. He also served one term as governor, and finally he

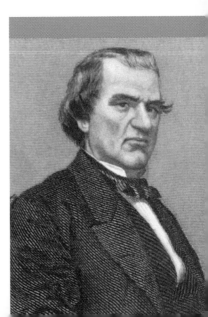

Andrew Johnson was the seventeenth President of the United States and the third from Tennessee. Johnson fought to keep Tennessee in the Union, gaining the respect of East Tennesseans and the hatred of West Tennesseans, who wanted to secede.

served as a United States senator from 1857 to 1862. All of these positions solidified Johnson's popularity in Tennessee.

But Johnson began to lose popularity as disputes between the North and the South heated up. Much of the disagreement was over slavery. The North wanted to outlaw slave labor, but the economy of the South was dependent on it. The South made plans to form its own government, which its citizens called the Confederacy.

Johnson had kept slaves on his plantation property and did not oppose slavery. What bothered Johnson was the South's desire to secede, or withdraw, from the Union. Johnson was the only Southern senator who refused to support secession. Partly because of Johnson's stubbornness, Tennessee was the last state to secede.

Because of its position as a border state, more Civil War battles were fought in Tennessee than any other state except Virginia. Tennessee proved itself to be the Volunteer State once again, but this time many of the state's volunteers were fighting against each other. About 70,000 Tennesseans fought for the Union— including about 20,000 African Americans who were fighting for their freedom. About 125,000 Tennessee soldiers fought for the Confederacy.

President Abraham Lincoln appointed Senator Andrew Johnson military governor of Tennessee in 1862. Because Lincoln was unpopular in the South, the Republicans wanted to team him with a Southern Democrat for his reelection bid in 1864. The party chose Andrew Johnson to be Lincoln's running mate.

Thus in 1865, Johnson became Vice President of the United States.

Confederate General Robert E. Lee surrendered in April 1865. Most people were relieved that the war was over, but many former Confederates were bitter. On April 14, 1865, John Wilkes Booth took out his bitterness on President Lincoln by shooting him dead in Ford's Theater in Washington, D.C. Andrew Johnson took over as President the next day.

The last state to leave the Union, Tennessee was also the first state to be readmitted, on July 24, 1866. The years that followed the Civil War, called Reconstruction, were rough for the South. There was a lot of work to be done. The South's economy was in shambles. Roads, farms, railroads, and factories needed to be rebuilt.

A group called the Radical Republicans, who took office across the South, wanted to punish all former Confederates severely. The Radicals in Tennessee brought forth many changes. For example, the right to vote was removed entirely from many former Confederates. At the same time, African Americans were given the right to vote. Former Confederates across the South were soon fed up with the Radical Republicans empowering African Americans while they themselves lost power. In Tennessee a secret

Confederate and Union soldiers in Tennessee posed together under one flag after the Civil War.

William G. Brownlow, a Radical Republican, was Tennessee's governor from 1865 to 1869. Brownlow was one of the Radical Republicans who held power in the South during Reconstruction.

group called the Ku Klux Klan (KKK) was formed to destroy Radical Republican political power. The KKK was organized in Tennessee in 1866. Its members put on white robes and hoods at night and terrorized African Americans and their sympathizers. The group spread throughout Tennessee and other southern states. Many African Americans were killed by KKK members. When most Radical Republicans were voted out of office in 1869, many people believed that the KKK kept African Americans away from the polls. The federal government passed laws designed to suppress the KKK, but the organization never completely died.

Recovery from the war was slow in Tennessee. Farmers didn't regain full production until the 1890s. Tennessee turned to manufacturing to make money. Factories and mills began producing everything from sweaters to flour. Coal mining also helped lead the state's economy toward recovery.

In 1917 the Volunteer State sent almost one hundred thousand soldiers to fight in World War I. Tennessee factories turned out war necessities such as gunpowder and cloth. The state's economy was flourishing.

In 1925 a high school science teacher in Dayton, Tennessee, named John Scopes was brought to trial by the state for teaching his students the theory of evolution. State law prohibited the teaching of evolution in the state's public school system. Evolution is the theory that humans developed from primitive beings related to apes and monkeys. The theory had been scientifically accepted since the late 1800s, but it offended some religious groups. Two of the country's greatest lawyers were brought in to try the case. William Jennings Bryan was the prosecuting attorney, and Clarence Darrow was the defense attorney. Scopes lost and was fined one hundred dollars. Teachers could not teach the theory of evolution until 1967.

In the 1930s the nation was struck by a severe economic slump called the Great Depression. Partly to help Tennessee's economy, the federal government formed the Tennessee Valley Authority (TVA). This organization developed the resources around the Tennessee River and provided jobs for Tennesseans at the same time. The TVA built dams and roads. It brought cheap electrical power and water to most parts of the state. The TVA, which continues to run these projects, also enriches the nation with energy research.

When the country entered World War II in 1941, Tennessee sent well over three hundred thousand men and women. The state was also involved in a top-secret project that had a major impact on the outcome of the war. In 1942 scientists in Oak Ridge, Tennessee, began work on the Manhattan Project, a government project to build an atomic bomb. The

above. Lawyer William Jennings Bryan argued against teaching evolution in the "Scopes Monkey Trial." Bryan died a few weeks after the end of the trial.

below. The Norris Dam, one of the many dams built by the Tennessee Valley Authority, provides energy, controls floods, and helps conserve soil and water.

project was so secret that most Oak Ridge residents didn't find out about it until August 1945, when the United States dropped the world's first atomic bomb on Hiroshima, Japan. Three days later another bomb was dropped on Nagasaki, bringing the war to an abrupt halt.

After World War II, one of Tennessee's—and the nation's—most important battles was for civil rights. The fight for civil rights was a fight to ensure equal opportunities for people of all races. In 1954 the United States Supreme Court ruled that public schools across the nation had to be desegregated. This meant that there could no longer be separate schools for African Americans and others. Tennessee began desegregation of its schools two years later.

On April 4, 1968, Dr. Martin Luther King, Jr., was assassinated in Memphis. Dr. King was an African American minister who was widely respected for his accomplishments and leadership in nonviolent social change. Riots broke out in many African American neighborhoods across the United States in the days that followed the assassination.

The 1980s brought important economic developments to the state. Chattanooga was one of several areas in the state that attracted more tourists than before. Chattanooga's leaders started to promote visiting their Civil War battlefields.

In 1968 Dr. Martin Luther King, Jr., was assassinated in Memphis while supporting a strike of African American sanitation workers. Here, hundreds of mourners accompany his casket.

The theme of the 1982 Knoxville World's Fair—"Energy Turns the World"—was represented by the gold-domed structure in the left foreground called the Sunsphere.

Knoxville hosted a World's Fair in 1982. Over 11 million people attended, boosting Tennessee's tourist industry. In 1985 a canal called the Tennessee-Tombigbee Waterway was completed. This canal has helped the state's industry and trade by connecting the Tennessee River to the Tombigbee River, which flows to the Gulf of Mexico. Another economic boost came from car manufacturing plants that were built across the state in the 1980s and 1990s.

Among Tennessee's most exciting developments in the 1990s were its educational reform programs. Tennessee started a project called the Twenty-First Century Schools. This was the first program in the nation to bring computer technology into the public schools. The program shows that the spirit of progress has taken hold in Tennessee. By influencing young people with programs like these, the state is hoping that the spirit will continue into the twenty-first century.

A Gift of History

Author Alex Haley remembered his childhood in Henning, Tennessee, very fondly. "On Saturday mornings, like now, an old man would come . . . and sit on an upturned Coke bottle—I mean a Coke, a wooden carton—right about there. And he would just sit and bend over like that. And a little crowd would start gathering. And he would stay there and the crowd would get a little bigger. Around 10:30 in the morning, his hand would go out for the first time, and he caught a fly . . . what fantastic reflexes. And he would, every Saturday, get crowds to watch him snatch a fly."

Before television, people found many ways to entertain themselves in a small town like Henning. They also found many ways to dream. Alex Haley captured some of these Tennessee dreams in his book called *Roots: The Saga of an American Family,* first published in 1976. But his book also reached much further back than his childhood in Tennessee. For twelve years, Haley researched his family ancestry, tracing it to Gambia, now a tiny country in western Africa.

Roots won a Pulitzer Prize in 1977. That same year, the book was made into a television miniseries. More than 130 million people, the largest television audience in history at the time, tuned in to the eight-part miniseries. Haley was famous. He could go wherever he wanted. But he chose to return to Tennessee, where he bought a 125-acre farm in a town called Norris.

Haley remembered his childhood dreams of leaving Henning, Tennessee.

This photo is taken from Roots, *the television movie based on Haley's book.* Roots *tells the story of Haley's family history from the time that his ancestor Kunta Kinte was taken from Gambia, West Africa, and sold as a slave in the South.*

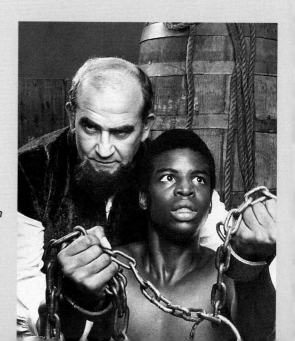

Alex Haley's boyhood home in Henning has been converted into a museum that preserves the feel of the 1920s of Haley's youth.

Alex Haley edited The Autobiography of Malcolm X.

"These train tracks. Nothing about this town, Henning, Tennessee, is more integral to its history, to my image of it, my memory of it, because these tracks were the link with the outside world," recalled Haley. "When the train would leave we would all run up and get right behind it, safely behind it, and we would run in the center of the track . . . for maybe a mile as the train chuffed, chuffed, picked up speed, and went on its way to Memphis or back this way to New Orleans or Chicago. And we would, as we ran, dream that one day we would grow up and be able to get enough money to buy us a ticket to go north and do good."

Alex Haley got much more than a ticket north. He received worldwide acclaim. *Roots* has been translated into more than thirty languages, and just the hardcover version of the book sold well over seven million copies.

Haley died in 1992, but he is not soon to be forgotten. His childhood home in Henning is now the Alex Haley House Museum. His farm in Norris has been purchased by the Children's Defense Fund to be used as a retreat and a conference center. But Haley has left more than land as a legacy.

"*Roots* is all of our stories," said Haley. "When you start talking about family, about lineage and ancestry, you are talking about every person on earth." Alex Haley's most important legacy is the gift of history.

An Economic Model for the Nation

The land of Tennessee is rich. The soil of the farmlands is fertile, the minerals are plentiful, and the forests are beautiful and full of wildlife. People who are born in Tennessee usually don't want to leave.

These days most Tennesseans don't have to leave. Industries are thriving, especially industries that involve manufacturing. In fact, Tennessee is one of only a few states in which manufacturing is growing rather than shrinking. Between 1982 and 1992, Tennessee's manufacturing grew by almost 45,000 jobs. Today over 20 percent of the workers in Tennessee have manufacturing jobs.

Tennessee's most important manufactured products are industrial and commercial machinery. Over twenty percent of the state's manufacturing income is made by producing engines, machine parts, and equipment for both heating and refrigeration.

Chemical manufacturing makes up almost ten percent of the state's manufacturing income. About

Tennessee's growth in manufacturing is a reflection of its hard-working people.

This is a farm in the Sequatchie Valley, north of Chattanooga. Cattle are Tennessee's leading farm product.

forty thousand workers in Tennessee help manufacture items such as paint, plastic, medicine, and soap. They also make chemicals for farms and for industry.

Tennessee's greatest manufacturing growth in the past few decades has been in transportation equipment. New automobile manufacturing plants have been a major contribution to this industry. Nissan and Toyota are in Rutherford County, just south of Nashville. Saturn cars are made in Spring Hill in Maury County. But cars aren't the only transportation equipment Tennessee workers help build. Boat, airplane, and bicycle manufacturers are also located in the state.

Three quarters of Tennessee's counties make fabricated metal products, the fourth largest manufacturing industry in Tennessee. The metalworking industry produces almost nine percent of the state's manufacturing income, making such items as cans, hardware, construction materials, and wire.

Tennessee is certainly not overrun with factories, however. Agriculture is still an important part of life. Almost half of the state is covered by farmland. Agriculture accounts for about two percent of the value of goods produced in the state, for a total of about $1.8 billion. More than half of that income comes from livestock. Tennessee farmers raise beef cattle, dairy cattle, and hogs. They also raise chickens for meat and for eggs.

Perhaps the most glamorous Tennessee farm product is the Tennessee Walking Horse, raised in the rolling hillsides of the Nashville Basin. First bred in 1935, this graceful horse is favored for its smooth gait. As the name implies, walking horses are raised by people who ride horses for pleasure. They are not used for labor or racing.

Tennessee's four largest cash crops are soybeans, tobacco, cotton, and corn. Tennessee's farmers also grow truck crops, such as apples, tomatoes, and snap beans. Truck crops are fruits and vegetables that are transported to local markets.

Mining is an important industry in parts of Tennessee, although it accounts for less than one percent of the value of goods produced in the state. Coal is the most valuable mineral. Zinc is also important. In fact, Tennessee mines more zinc than any

Most of Tennessee's tobacco is grown at the northern border, near Kentucky and Virginia.

other state. Tennessee is also a leader in the mining of crushed stone, used mostly for roads. Many of the nation's—and even the world's—roads have a bit of Tennessee in them.

Tennessee, like most other states, relies on service industries for a large part of its income. Service industries do not manufacture a product. They are businesses that provide goods for people or perform tasks for them. Service industries include many areas, such as trade, banking, communications, and government. Well over 1.5 million Tennesseans work in service industries.

Tennessee's most important area of service industries is trade. Retail trade is the selling of a small number of goods directly to consumers. Clothing and gift stores are examples of retail trade. Wholesale trade is the selling of large quantities of goods, usually to

Tennessee's service industry includes high-tech companies, such as St. Jude Children's Research Hospital in Memphis.

companies. Both wholesale and retail trade are important industries in Nashville and Memphis.

These two cities also play large roles in Tennessee's
second-ranking service industry, personal and community services. Doctors, nurses, clerical workers, restau-
rant workers, and lawyers all fall into this category.
The third category is made up of the finance, insurance, and real estate businesses. These services pro-
duce almost ten billion dollars for Tennessee each
year. Nashville and Memphis lead once again in this
area. Nashville has the most banks in the state, while
Memphis is the home of the state's largest bank.

Another division of Tennessee's service industries
is related to natural resources. That is because the
beauty of the state's resources is linked to the tourism
industry. Eight million tourists come to the state every
year to visit the Great Smoky Mountains National
Park or Cherokee National Forest. Music, however,
is the state's biggest tourist draw. Nashville is the
"Country Music Capital of the World," bringing
countless tourists. And Memphis is the home of
Graceland, Elvis Presley's mansion, which draws about
six hundred thousand visitors to the state each year.

Tennessee is a modern-day economic success story.
In the first half of the 1990s, Tennessee's economy and
government financial management has been consis-
tently ranked in the top ten by magazines such as
Financial World and *U.S. News and World Report*.
Tennessee knows how to do business, and it doesn't
mind at all being compared to others as a model of
success.

Memphis is the headquar-
ters for the Federal Express
Corporation, and also serves
as one of the regional distribution hubs.

New Places for an Old Industry

Where are cars made in this country? The automatic answer to that question used to be "Detroit" or at least "the Midwest." That's not true any longer, however. These days, one answer is "Tennessee." Not all cars are made in Tennessee, of course, but more and more automobile plants and their suppliers are located here.

One reason so many new automobile factories have located in Tennessee is that the people here have enthusiastically joined the revolution in manufacturing that has taken place in recent years. This change in the way things are done demands more of employees. At the same time, it provides them with an important voice in their own work and that of their company.

The new plants have provided many new jobs for the people of Tennessee. Gary Montgomery was very happy about it. "I always wanted to work in an automotive plant because of the pay, also because of the benefits. And I'd see it on TV and I'd say,

'Hey, you know, that's really neat. . . . I'd like to work there.' But I wasn't willing to move. I wanted to stay in the community that I grew up in." Gary finally got his chance to have it both ways, when he started to work at a new automobile plant in Smyrna.

The new jobs have provided more than good pay and benefits. They've provided a real challenge and some opportunities that people like Gary never dreamed of. Some employees of an automobile parts company in Portland, for example, have found themselves traveling to Japan for several months of training at their company's headquarters plant.

Others have participated in developing ways to cut time and increase productivity. One manufacturing plant in Ripley was so successful that it doubled its output without increasing its costs!

Another automobile-supply factory in Tennessee operates in a truly unique way. In order to use its machinery and facilities enough to justify their cost, the factory must operate 24 hours a day. So its employees have developed a totally different style of working that reinvented the work week. They work 12-hour shifts on a peculiar but efficient schedule. They work two days, have two days off, work three days, have two days off, then work two days followed by three days off. Then they start the cycle all over again. They build tires in a whole new way. And the system works so well that the company is beginning to use it in all its plants.

When it comes to new ideas, the automobile industry and the people of Tennessee are a terrific combination.

When Saturn built its plant in Spring Hill, Tennessee, the project brought an investment of $1.9 billion to the state. And that was before a single automobile was ever built!

This assembly line is part of the Nissan plant in Smyrna.

CULTURE

Homemade in Tennessee

There is a homemade tradition in Tennessee, where craftspeople still use methods passed down over many generations. They make quilts out of cloth scraps, wooden toys from backyard trees, and banjos from ham cans. Many Tennessee artists follow in that tradition, making music and literature out of the history and spirit of their state.

One fine example is John Crowe Ransom, a poet and literary critic from Pulaski, Tennessee. While at Vanderbilt University in Nashville shortly after World War I, Ransom formed a group of writers called the Fugitives. The Fugitives included well-known writers Robert Penn Warren and Allen Tate, who centered their work and beliefs around their southern heritage. They attacked the rapid industrial growth of the area and spoke out in favor of a return to the agricultural society of the Old South.

Another Tennessee native, writer James Agee, also shaped his works from his experiences in the South. Agee completed his first major success in 1941 with

Beale Street in Memphis has been synonymous with blues, rock 'n' roll, and music of all kinds for almost a hundred years.

Let Us Now Praise Famous Men. In 1958 his novel *A Death in the Family* won the Pulitzer Prize. The play he based on the novel, *All the Way Home*, won a Pulitzer in 1961. Agee also wrote many screenplays for films, such as *The African Queen*, starring Katharine Hepburn and Humphrey Bogart. But his best work was based on life in the South where he grew up.

Some people may argue that Tennessee's musicians have captured the spirit of the South like no other art form has. Tennessee, most notably Nashville and Memphis, is the unofficial home of many of today's musical styles. Country music certainly is represented in Nashville, the home of the Grand Ole Opry. Many country singers and musicians achieved fame after appearing on the Opry stage.

W. C. Handy, the Father of the Blues, popularized music known as "the blues" from folk songs and African American church songs. He was the first person to put many of these traditional songs down on paper. Born in Alabama, Handy came to Beale Street in Memphis in 1908. He soon formed a band and began to compose and perform the music that would make him—and Beale Street—famous. Despite becoming partially blind, W. C. Handy continued to conduct his own band until he was nearly fifty.

A few years after W. C. Handy came to Memphis, a Chattanooga-born blues singer added her talent to the Beale Street blues. Her name was Bessie

Smith. She was called the Empress of the Blues. Smith made her first recording in Memphis when she was 25 years old. She also wrote over 150 songs and performed with famous band leaders Louis Armstrong, Benny Goodman, and others.

Elvis Aron Presley borrowed from Beale Street blues, mixed it with the country music and gospel music of his childhood, and came up with a totally unique sound—rock 'n' roll. Presley was born in Mississippi but he was raised in Memphis. In 1954, at age nineteen, he made his first recording at a Memphis recording studio called Sun Records. From there he went on to record 45 gold records and star in 33 films. Presley sold an astounding five hundred million records in his lifetime. Although he died in 1977, well over a half-million fans each year still visit Graceland, his home in Memphis.

Sun Records in Memphis recorded dozens of other musicians in the 1950s. Many of these musicians were unknown at the time, outside of a small circle of friends. B. B. King, Muddy Waters, Jerry Lee Lewis, Roy Orbison, and Johnny Cash, to name a few, became national idols after signing a Sun Records contract.

Aretha Franklin moved away from Memphis at a very early age. But it is evident from her singing that Memphis music made an impression on her before she left. Franklin combined blues, gospel, and

Bessie Smith's 1923 recording, "Down Hearted Blues," sold over two million copies.

Elvis Presley's home, Graceland, provides the background for this photo of his pink 1954 Fleetwood Cadillac.

rock influences to create a style that crowned her the Queen of Soul. Singer Tina Turner performs a style known as rhythm and blues, which is really a mix of the many styles that were cultivated in Memphis. Turner was born and raised in Nutbush, Tennessee, but it was Memphis music that helped her become the Grammy award-winning star she is today.

Memphis also has some of the best and most original museums in the nation. The Pink Palace Museum and Planetarium, for example, displays both the natural and the cultural histories of Tennessee and the middle-South. The Mississippi River Museum features the history of the river and the people who explored it or somehow linked it to their fame. Visitors can splash through a scale model of the Mississippi River or board a restored nineteenth-century riverboat. Memphis is also the home of the National Civil Rights Museum. It was built on the site of the 1968 assassination of

Dr. Martin Luther King, Jr. The museum illustrates, through displays and exhibits, the sights, the sounds, and the tensions of the American civil rights movement.

Nashville also has many fine museums as well as historical sites. A full-size replica of the Parthenon in Athens, Greece, was built in Centennial Park to reflect the city's reputation as the "Athens of the South." Nashville's model of the original Greek Parthenon houses marble sculptures and the city's permanent collection of fine paintings. Another museum, the Hermitage, was once the home of the nation's seventh President, Andrew Jackson.

The Parthenon in Nashville is the world's only full-size replica of the Parthenon in Athens, Greece.

Tennessee's culture is marked by the ability of its artists to borrow from the original and create something new. Whatever the art form, from toys to toe-tapping music, the final product always carries a stamp that proudly says "Made in Tennessee."

Tourism is crucial to the economy of Memphis. Here, children play in a scale model of the Mississippi, part of the Mississippi River Museum.

Sweet Country Music

"Diane, this is an old fiddle tune that I want you to learn to play. It's called 'Did You Ever See the Devil, Uncle Joe?' . . . I learned it from an old fiddle player when I was your age. And I want you to listen to me play it. I want you to learn to play it. And I want to hear you play it."

At the Smithville Jamboree, fiddler Frazier Moss passes on an old tune to a young fiddler. That scene has been repeated in these mountains for generations. Just as the people of Tennessee made their own clothes and

The Fiddler's Jamboree in Smithville, Tennessee, is held each year on Fourth of July Weekend.

tools, they made their own music. And they still make it, in Smithville and in Nashville.

"I knew that I was addicted to music," said country singer Wynonna Judd. "I knew that I loved it and every time I heard a new song it excited me. I think it wasn't till I was in tenth grade of high school . . . I performed in front of my school at the talent show and I won it. I got real excited . . . so it wasn't till then that I decided I really wanted to start doing it."

Wynonna Judd's mother, Naomi, didn't let her try to make it in the big time until she finished high school. But after Wynonna's graduation, both of them started working on the dream. They started singing together, using the close harmonies of traditional Tennessee music. And they started looking for a break. Naomi Judd describes how they struggled just before they had success.

"During the last five years, I supported the two kids and myself making a living as a registered nurse in the Williamson County Hospital down where we lived. I was taking care of a young girl whose father was one of Nashville's top producers, Brent Maher. I became satisfied that he was the man. So on my day off from the

The Ryman Auditorium was the home of the Grand Ole Opry for more than thirty years.

37

hospital, I put my best dress on and went in and took him a tape."

The rest, as they say, is history. Brent Maher worked with the Judds and produced their first record, "Mama, He's Crazy." They have since had many hit songs, recorded many albums, and made a number of music videos.

The Judds are only two of the many performers to become famous out of Nashville. For country music performers, one of the highest achievements is performing in the Grand Ole Opry in Nashville.

And while the hits keep rolling out of Nashville, the music keeps rolling out of the hills of Tennessee. The banjo players and fiddlers keep playing. And the music is passed on for another generation.

Musicians perform at the Grand Ole Opry. WSM, the name of the radio station that broadcasts the Opry, stands for "We Shield Millions." This was the motto of the insurance company that first funded the station.

Patsy Cline was one of the singers who made the Nashville Sound famous in the 1950s and 1960s. Here, she performs in the Grand Ole Opry in the Ryman Auditorium.

The Grand Ole Opry doesn't have a monopoly on all of Tennessee's country music talent.

A Place to Remember

John Rice Irwin has gadgets and guitars and old shoes at his Museum of Appalachia in Norris, Tennessee. Here is the evidence of a way of life. Here the great-great-grandchildren of the pioneers are reminded of how their ancestors lived in the early days of Tennessee.

"They had to make their own clothing, their own shoes," said Irwin. "They had to be their own blacksmiths and make their own wagons and everything that had to be done, they had to do themselves. They couldn't go to the supermarket and buy it. In Appalachia, it was a little more that way because you had people who were so isolated."

John Rice Irwin's family had been in this region for two hundred years when he decided to start the museum in the late 1960s. The first things to go into his collection were given to him by his grandfather. Now, there are more than two hundred thousand items.

The museum has grown to 65 acres, with authentic log buildings, a gift shop, an auditorium, and two museum buildings. All these buildings were made by hand from the floors to the shingles, just the way they used to be made. Irwin also raises sheep and crops at his museum. Special events feature traditional activities such as rail

This is the inside of one of the authentic log cabins of the Museum of Appalachia. This building was filmed as Daniel Boone's home in a television series.

John Rice Irwin strums a mandolin in the Museum of Appalachia.

splitting and molasses boiling. Irwin says he strives to make the grounds "appear as though the family had just strolled down to the spring to fetch the daily supply of water."

The Museum of Appalachia has been praised from coast to coast, with rave reviews from the *New York Times* to the *Los Angeles Herald Examiner.* But John Rice Irwin doesn't care much about that. Irwin is simply glad to help the people of Appalachia understand and be proud of their heritage.

As Irwin says, "There's so many people that Tennessee has produced that were what I think were great people. People that I would consider to be great you never heard of because they lived on a little farm and spent their life there. I feel sort of an obligation to try to tell their grandsons and their great-grandsons and so forth how it was. And if they see some of the things—the pair of shoes that Uncle

Workers lead plow horses at the Museum of Appalachia.

Camel wore for 24 years and how he patched them and so forth—they might get a little bit of appreciation of him and the contributions he made."

41

Tomorrow's Tennessee

The people of Tennessee have proven themselves unafraid of progress and the future, while they continue to place high value on tradition. The old is not replaced; instead it is skillfully incorporated into the new.

Tennessee's cities are proof of this level-headed progress. Memphis is one of the best examples. The city has proudly maintained historic Beale Street and other districts, while also adding a new $70 million arena nearby. The 32-story pyramid arena is a striking symbol for the future, housing sports, business, and entertainment events. Nashville has also completed a new 20,000-seat arena, and in 1994 it added a new skyscraper to the city's skyline.

Chattanooga is also modernizing. A multimillion dollar program to bring new life to the downtown area is scheduled to extend into the twenty-first century. New facilities include a children's museum, a 12-story aquarium, and an extensive riverfront renovation that has gained national acclaim.

The Pyramid in Memphis is the third largest pyramid in the world. This futuristic sports arena has a base the size of six football fields.

Nashville is the capital of Tennessee, country music, and much of the state's business expansion.

Tennessee's plans always include tomorrow's leaders. Education has become a main focus of the state. In fact, nearly half of Tennessee's tax money is funneled into education programs. Investments such as the Twenty-First Century Schools Program see to it that Tennessee's students won't be left behind in this age of expanding technology. Tennessee schools have equipped four thousand classrooms with the latest computer technology. More expansions are in the works.

Tennessee is also well-prepared to join the global economy. Nearly 150 of the world's 500 largest companies have manufacturing facilities in Tennessee. In addition, the state has formed a partnership of business, education, and governmental agencies called Tennessee Tomorrow, Inc. This partnership will ensure that Tennessee's businesses stay involved as the nation expands its trade to more nations.

The first half of the 1990s brought Tennessee multiple top-ten rankings for economic and financial health. With such a clear vision for the future, and so much solid ground to build on, Tennessee can only move forward.

Important Historical Events

1540 Spanish explorer Hernando de Soto leads an expedition into the Tennessee River valley.

1673 French and English explorers chart the Tennessee region.

1763 The Treaty of Paris is signed, ending the French and Indian War.

1772 Settlers in the Tennessee wilderness set up an independent government called the Watauga Association.

1775 The Transylvania Land Company buys large amounts of land from the Cherokee, including Tennessee and Kentucky. Daniel Boone blazes a trail known as the Wilderness Road.

1779 Jonesborough becomes the first chartered town in Tennessee. Fort Nashborough, the future site of Nashville, is built on the Cumberland River.

1784 Three counties in eastern Tennessee rebel against North Carolina and create their own state called Franklin.

1789 The federal government takes over North Carolina's Tennessee territory, naming it the Territory of the United States South of the River Ohio.

1796 Tennessee becomes the sixteenth state on June 1. The capital is Knoxville.

1821 The Cherokee adopt a new alphabet created by Sequoyah.

1828 Andrew Jackson of Tennessee is elected the seventh President of the United States.

1830 Jackson signs the Indian Removal Act.

1838 Native Americans are forced out of Tennessee and other parts of the South on the Trail of Tears.

1843 Nashville becomes Tennessee's permanent state capital.

1845 Tennessean James K. Polk becomes the eleventh President of the United States.

1861 Tennessee is the last state to join the Confederate States of America. The Civil War begins.

1862 President Abraham Lincoln appoints Andrew Johnson military governor of Tennessee.

1865 Andrew Johnson becomes the seventeenth President of the United States after President Lincoln is assassinated.

1866 Tennessee is the first Confederate state to be readmitted to the Union. The Ku Klux Klan is founded in Pulaski.

1925 The decision on the "Scopes Monkey Trial" upholds the ban on teaching the theory of evolution in public schools. The Grand Ole Opry radio show begins broadcasting from Nashville.

1933 Congress creates the Tennessee Valley Authority.

1942 The Oak Ridge atomic energy plant is built by the federal government.

1968 Civil rights leader Dr. Martin Luther King, Jr., is assassinated in Memphis.

1982 Knoxville hosts the World's Fair. Nissan opens the area's first auto plant in Smyrna.

1985 The Tennessee-Tombigbee Waterway is completed.

1991 Tennessee adopts the Twenty-First Century Schools Program to prepare students for the nation's technological future.

Tennessee's state flag was adopted in 1905. The three stars represent the state's three major regions: West, Middle, and East Tennessee.

Tennessee Almanac

Nicknames. The Volunteer State, The Big Bend State

Capital. Nashville

State Bird. Mockingbird

State Flower. Iris

State Tree. Tulip poplar

State Motto. Agriculture and Commerce

State Songs. "The Tennessee Waltz," "Rocky Top"

State Abbreviations. Tenn. (traditional); TN (postal)

Statehood. June 1, 1796, the 16th state

Government. Congress: U.S. senators, 2; U.S. representatives, 9. State Legislature: senators, 33; representatives, 99. Counties: 95

Area. 42,146 sq mi (109,158 sq km), 34th in size among the states

Greatest Distances. north/south, 116 mi (187 km); east/west, 482 mi (775 km)

Elevation. Highest: Clingmans Dome, 6,643 ft (2,025 m). Lowest: 182 ft (55 m)

Population. 1990 Census: 4,896,641 (7% increase over 1980), 17th among the states. Density: 116 persons per sq mi (45 persons per sq km). Distribution: 61% urban, 39% rural. 1980 Census: 4,591,120

Economy. *Agriculture*: beef and dairy cattle, hogs, chickens, soybeans, tobacco, cotton, corn. *Manufacturing*: industrial and commercial machinery, chemicals, transportation equipment, fabricated metal products. *Mining*: coal, zinc, crushed stone

State Seal

State Bird: Mockingbird

State Flower: Iris

Annual Events

★ Elvis Presley's Birthday Celebration at Graceland in Memphis (January)

★ Tennessee Old-Time Fiddlers Championship in Clarksville (March)

★ Memphis in May International Festival (May)

★ Fiddler's Jamboree and Crafts Festival in Smithville (June)

★ Nashville's International Country Music Fan Fair (Fourth of July Weekend)

★ Cherokee Days of Recognition in Cleveland (August)

★ Tennessee State Fair in Nashville (September)

★ Fall Homecoming at the Museum of Appalachia in Norris (October)

★ National Storytelling Festival in Jonesborough (October)

★ Liberty Bowl Football Game in Memphis (December)

Places to Visit

★ American Museum of Science and Energy in Oak Ridge

★ Beale Street and Graceland in Memphis

★ Casey Jones Home and Railroad Museum in Jackson

★ Cherokee National Forest and Great Smoky Mountains National Park in eastern Tennessee

★ The Hermitage, near Nashville

★ Lost Sea Caverns in Sweetwater

★ National Civil Rights Museum in Memphis

★ Opryland USA and the Ryman Auditorium in Nashville

★ The Parthenon in Nashville

★ The Peabody Ducks at the Peabody Hotel in Memphis

★ Tennessee Aquarium in Chattanooga